☐ ק ו' - כֵּיצַד מְבָרְכִין - מִשְׁנָה א' ☐

1) How do we say the *brocha* on fruits?	כֵּיצַד מְבָרְכִין עַל הַפֵּרוֹת? (1
2) On fruits of the tree he says,	עַל פֵּרוֹת הָאִילָן אוֹמֵר, (2
3) "...the Creator of the fruit of the tree,"	"בּוֹרֵא פְּרִי הָעֵץ," (3
4) aside from wine	חוּץ מִן הַיַּיִן (4
5) because on wine he says,	שֶׁעַל הַיַּיִן אוֹמֵר, (5
6) "...the Creator of the fruit of the vine."	"בּוֹרֵא פְּרִי הַגָּפֶן." (6
7) And on fruits of the earth he says,	וְעַל פֵּרוֹת הָאָרֶץ אוֹמֵר, (7
8) "...the Creator of the fruit of the ground,"	"בּוֹרֵא פְּרִי הָאֲדָמָה," (8
9) aside from bread	חוּץ מִן הַפַּת (9
10) because on bread he says,	שֶׁעַל הַפַּת הוּא אוֹמֵר, (10
11) "...Who brings bread from the earth."	"הַמּוֹצִיא לֶחֶם מִן הָאָרֶץ." (11
12) And on vegetables◇ he says,	וְעַל הַיְרָקוֹת אוֹמֵר, (12
13) "...the Creator of the fruit of the ground."	"בּוֹרֵא פְּרִי הָאֲדָמָה." (13
14) Rabbe Yehuda says,	רַבִּי יְהוּדָה אוֹמֵר, (14
15) "...the Creator of types of herbs."	"בּוֹרֵא מִינֵי דְשָׁאִים." (15

◇ *Like lettuce*

1. Is the הלכה to say a ברכה before eating מדאורייתא, (from the Torah) מדרבנן (from the Rabbis), or a מנהג (custom)? _____

2. Why did the חכמים make a special ברכה for wine and bread? _____
_____

3. What is the ברכה on pineapples and bananas? _____

4. Bananas grow on a tree. Why isn't their ברכה a "בורא פרי העץ"? _____
_____

☐ בְּרָכוֹת פֶּרֶק ו' - כֵּיצַד מְבָרְכִין - מִשְׁנָה ב' ☐

1) (If) he said the *brocha* on fruits of the tree,   בַּרַךְ עַל פֵּירוֹת הָאִילָן, (1

2) "...the Creator of the fruit of the ground,"   "בּוֹרֵא פְּרִי הָאֲדָמָה," (2

3) he fulfilled his obligation.   יָצָא. (3

4) and (if) on fruits of the earth,   וְעַל פֵּירוֹת הָאָרֶץ, (4

5) "...the Creator of the fruit of the trees,"   "בּוֹרֵא פְּרִי הָעֵץ," (5

6) he has not fulfilled his obligation.   לֹא יָצָא. (6

7) On all of them   עַל כֻּלָּם (7

8) if he said,   אִם אָמַר, (8

9) "*shehakol nee'yeh*,"   "שֶׁהַכֹּל נִהְיָה," (9

10) he fulfilled his obligation.   יָצָא. (10

---

1. Please write two Herew words for "tree". _____

2. Why would a person be יוֹצֵא if he said a בּוֹרֵא פְּרִי הָאדמה on the fruit of a tree? _____

   _____

3. Why would a person not be יוֹצֵא if he said a בּוֹרֵא פְּרִי העץ on the produce of the earth? ____

   _____

4. If a person said a שהכל on bread or wine, would he be יוֹצֵא? _____

5. According to הלכה, if you do not know which ברכה to say, is it permissible to "just say a שהכל?"

   _____

6. Chaim is at home by himself. He would like to eat a banana, but does not know if he should say a

   האדמה or a העץ. Please write a suggestion which will enable him to eat the banana. _____

   _____

7. Please write another suggestion for him. _____

בּוֹרֵא
פְּרִי הָאֲדָמָה

⊟ ברכות פרק ו' - כיצד מברכין - משנה ג' ⊟

1) On anything whose growth isn't from the earth	(1 עַל דָּבָר שֶׁאֵינוֹ גְּדוּלוֹ מִן הָאָרֶץ
2) he says,	(2 אוֹמֵר,
3) "shehakol."	(3 "שֶׁהַכֹּל."
4) On vinegar,	(4 עַל הַחֹמֶץ,
5) and on fallen (unripe) fruits,	(5 וְעַל הַנּוֹבְלוֹת,
6) and on (kosher) locusts he says,	(6 וְעַל הַגּוֹבַאי אוֹמֵר,
7) "shehakol."	(7 "שֶׁהַכֹּל."
8) On milk, and on cheese,	(8 עַל הֶחָלָב, וְעַל הַגְּבִינָה,
9) and on eggs he says,	(9 וְעַל הַבֵּיצִים אוֹמֵר,
10) "shehakol."	(10 "שֶׁהַכֹּל."
11) Rabbe Yehuda says,	(11 רַבִּי יְהוּדָה אוֹמֵר,
12) "Anything which is a type of curse	(12 "כָּל שֶׁהוּא מִין קְלָלָה
13) we don't say a brocha on it."	(13 אֵין מְבָרְכִין עָלָיו."

1. What is the ברכה on mushrooms? _____
2. Why? _____
3. Why are נובלות a מין קללה? _____
_____
4. Why is vinegar considered a מין קללה? _____
_____
5. Why might locusts be considered a מין קללה? _____
_____
6. The practice of most Jews is not to eat any type of locusts. Why? _____

The ברכה on mushrooms is שהכל, since they are not nourished from the ground in the usual way.

☐ ברכות פרק ו׳ - כיצד מברכין - משנה ד׳ ☐

1) If there were in front of him	הָיוּ לְפָנָיו	(1
2) many types (of food),	מִינִים הַרְבֵּה,	(2
3) Rabbe Yehuda says,	רַבִּי יְהוּדָה אוֹמֵר,	(3
4) "If there is among them from the *seven species*	״אִם יֵשׁ בֵּינֵיהֶם מִמִּין שֶׁבַע	(4
5) he says the *brocha* on it."	מְבָרֵךְ עָלָיו.״	(5
6) And the Chachomim say,	וַחֲכָמִים אוֹמְרִים,	(6
7) "He says the *brocha*	״מְבָרֵךְ	(7
8) on whichever one he wants."	עַל אֵיזֶה מֵהֶם שֶׁיִּרְצֶה.״	(8

אֶרֶץ חִטָּה וּשְׂעֹרָה וְגֶפֶן וּתְאֵנָה וְרִמּוֹן, אֶרֶץ זֵית שֶׁמֶן וּדְבָשׁ.
דברים פרק ח׳ פסוק ח׳

The order of ברכות: (1 הַמּוֹצִיא, (2 מְזוֹנוֹת (3 הַגֶּפֶן, (4 הָעֵץ, (5 הָאֲדָמָה, (6 שֶׁהַכֹּל.

The order of בּוֹרֵא פְּרִי הָעֵץ: 1) olives, 2) dates, 3) grapes, 4) figs, 5) pomegranates, what you like best.

1. This פסוק mentions two types of grain. What are they? _____

2. We say that there are five special types of grain. How is it possible to have five special types of grain if there are only two in the list? _____

3. Please draw a line from each word to its translation.

olive (oil)	גפן
date (honey)	דבש
grapes(s)	זית שמן
fig(s)	תאנה
pomegranate(s)	רמון

4. According to the שלחן ערוך the הלכה is that a person should say the ברכה on the מין שבע even if he likes a different type of fruit more. If he is going to eat grapes, an apple, and a tangerine, on which should he say the ברכה? _____

5. If he is going to eat a pear, an apple, and a peach, how does he decide on which he should say the ברכה? _____

|:| ברכות פרק ו' - כיצד מברכין - משנה ה' |:|

1) (If) he said the *brocha* on the wine	1) בֵּרַךְ עַל הַיַּיִן
2) which is before the (food) meal,	2) שֶׁלִּפְנֵי הַמָּזוֹן,
3) he exempted# the wine	3) פָּטַר אֶת הַיַּיִן
4) which is after the (food) meal*.	4) שֶׁלְּאַחַר הַמָּזוֹן.
5) (If) he said the *brocha* on the appetizer^	5) בֵּרַךְ עַל הַפַּרְפֶּרֶת
6) which is before the (food) meal,	6) שֶׁלִּפְנֵי הַמָּזוֹן,
7) he exempted the dessert	7) פָּטַר אֶת הַפַּרְפֶּרֶת
8) which is after the (food) meal.	8) שֶׁלְּאַחַר הַמָּזוֹן.
9) (If) he said the *brocha* on the bread,	9) בֵּרַךְ עַל הַפַּת,
10) he exempted the appetizer.	10) פָּטַר אֶת הַפַּרְפֶּרֶת.
11) (But) on the appetizer, he did not exempt the bread.	11) עַל הַפַּרְפֶּרֶת, לֹא פָטַר אֶת הַפַּת.
12) Bais Shammai say,	12) בֵּית שַׁמַּאי אוֹמְרִים,
13) "Not even what is prepared in a pot."	13) "אַף לֹא מַעֲשֵׂה קְדֵרָה."

Fulfilled the obligation of saying a ברכה.

* But before ברכת המזון.

^ The פרפרת is a type of food made of grain, which can be eaten as an appetizer (before the meal), or as a desert after the meal.

---

1. If he made קידוש on wine, ate a meal, and said ברכת המזון, does he have to say a ברכה on the wine which he drinks after "bentching"? _____

2. Why might you think that the ברכה on the פרפרת should exempt the bread? [Remember, we said that the פרפרת is made of grain.] _____
_____

3. What is מַעֲשֵׂה קְדֵרָה? _____
_____

Make sure to say each ברכה in the proper order.

☐ ברכות פרק ו' - כיצד מברכין - משנה ו' ☐

1) (If) they were sitting to eat	הָיוּ יוֹשְׁבִין לֶאֱכֹל,	(1
2) each one says the *brocha* for himself.	כָּל אֶחָד וְאֶחָד מְבָרֵךְ לְעַצְמוֹ.	(2
3) If they reclined,	הֵסֵבּוּ,	(3
4) one says the *brocha* for all of them.	אֶחָד מְבָרֵךְ לְכוּלָן.	(4
5) (If) wine was brought to them during the meal,	בָּא לָהֶם יַיִן בְּתוֹךְ הַמָּזוֹן,	(5
6) each one says the *brocha* for himself;	כָּל אֶחָד וְאֶחָד מְבָרֵךְ לְעַצְמוֹ;	(6
7) (but) after the meal,^	לְאַחַר הַמָּזוֹן,	(7
8) one says the *brocha* for all of them.	אֶחָד מְבָרֵךְ לְכוּלָם.	(8
9) And he says the *brocha* on the spice,	וְהוּא אוֹמֵר עַל הַמוּגְמָר,	(9
10) even though they don't bring the spice in	אַף עַל פִּי שֶׁאֵין מְבִיאִין אֶת הַמוּגְמָר	(10
11) except after the meal.	אֶלָּא לְאַחַר הַסְעוּדָה.	(11

^ *If wine is brought after the meal.*

___

1. In the beginning of this משנה, what difference does it make if they sit down [without being organized], or if they recline at the meal? _____

_____

2. If they said, "נֵיזֵיל נֵיכוּל נַהֲמָא בְּדוּכְתָא פְּלָן" they are considered as if they are having an organized meal, even if they are not reclining. What does that expression mean? _____

_____

3. Which ברכה is this משנה speaking about [when it says one can be מברך for all of them]? _____

_____

4. Even if they are eating an organized meal together, if wine was brought in the middle of the meal, each person should say his own ברכה. Why? _____

_____

5. What could a person say, before saying the ברכה on the wine, in order to permit him to say the ברכה for everyone? _____

⊡ ברכות פרק ו' - כיצד מברכין - משנה ז' ⊡

1) If they brought in front of him salted [food]	1) הֵבִיאוּ לְפָנָיו מָלִיחַ
2) in the beginning ^	2) בַּתְּחִלָּה
3) and bread with it,	3) וּפַת עִמּוֹ
4) he says the *brocha* on the salted [food]	4) מְבָרֵךְ עַל הַמָּלִיחַ
5) and he exempts* the bread,	5) וּפוֹטֵר אֶת הַפַּת,
6) because the bread is secondary (less important) to it.	6) שֶׁהַפַּת טְפֵלָה לוֹ.
7) This is the rule:	7) זֶה הַכְּלָל:
8) anything which is a main [food]	8) כָּל שֶׁהוּא עִקָּר
9) and with it is something secondary,	9) וְעִמָּהּ טְפֵלָה,
10) he says the *brocha* on the main [food]	10) מְבָרֵךְ עַל הָעִקָּר
11) and he exempts the secondary [food].	11) וּפוֹטֵר אֶת הַטְּפֵלָה.

^ The salty food was brought before the bread, since the main intention is

to eat the salty food.

* This means that the ברכה on the main food will go on the secondary food too.

_____

1. What do we mean by "עיקר"? _____

2. What do we mean by "טפלה"? _____

3. Why is this person eating the bread? _____

_____

4. If he wants to eat the bread (which is the טפלה) and afterwards he will eat the salty food (which is

the עיקר), according to many opinions he must _____ .

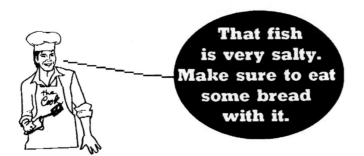

That fish
is very salty.
Make sure to eat
some bread
with it.

ברכות פרק ו' - כיצד מברכין - משנה ח'

1) "(If) he ate figs, grapes, or pomegranates,	(1 "אָכַל תְּאֵנִים, עֲנָבִים, וְרִמּוֹנִים,
2) he says after them *Three Blessings*,"	(2 מְבָרֵךְ אַחֲרֵיהֶם שָׁלֹשׁ בְּרָכוֹת,"
3) these are the words of Rabbon Gamliel.	(3 דִּבְרֵי רַבָּן גַּמְלִיאֵל.
4) And the Chachomim say,	(4 וַחֲכָמִים אוֹמְרִים,
5) "One *brocha* made from three."	(5 "בְּרָכָה אַחַת מֵעֵין שָׁלֹשׁ."
6) Rabbe Akiva says,	(6 רַבִּי עֲקִיבָא אוֹמֵר,
7) "Even if he ate boiled vegetables	(7 "אֲפִילוּ אָכַל שֶׁלֶק
8) and it is his food (for his meal)	(8 וְהוּא מְזוֹנוֹ
9) he says after it *Three Blessings*."	(9 מְבָרֵךְ אַחֲרָיו שָׁלֹשׁ בְּרָכוֹת."
10) One who drinks water for his thirst says,	(10 הַשּׁוֹתֶה מַיִם לִצְמָאוֹ אוֹמֵר,
11) "shehakol nee'yeh bid'va'ro."	(11 "שֶׁהַכֹּל נִהְיֶה בִּדְבָרוֹ."
12) Rabbe Tarfon says,	(12 רַבִּי טַרְפוֹן אוֹמֵר,
13) "bo'rai n'fa'shos rabbos."	(13 "בּוֹרֵא נְפָשׁוֹת רַבּוֹת."

---

1. How many ברכות are there in ברכת המזון? _____

2. If so, why is ברכת המזון called, "שָׁלֹשׁ בְּרָכוֹת"? _____
    _____

3. What is "בְּרָכָה אַחַת מֵעֵין שָׁלֹשׁ"? _____

4. Please write an example of drinking water which does not require any ברכה. _____
    _____

5. According to רבי טרפון, when is the ברכה of בּוֹרֵא נְפָשׁוֹת said? _____
    _____

DO YOU KNOW THE BROCHA ON EACH OF THESE ITEMS?

🔲 ברכות פרק ז' - שלשה שאכלו - הקדמה למשנה א' 🔲

The order of תרומות ומעשרות

- תרומה גדולה	One fiftieth of the produce, which is given to a Kohain.
- מעשר ראשון	One tenth of the produce, which is given to a Levi.
(תרומת מעשר) -	The Levi gives one tenth of what he received to a Kohain.
- מעשר שני	The owner of the produce takes one tenth of what remains. He must eat this in Yerushalayim, or redeem it so that he can purchase food to eat in Yerushalayim.
(מעשר עני) -	During the 3rd and 6th years of the 7 year shmitta cycle, the owner gives one tenth to the poor people - instead of eating it in Yerushalayim.

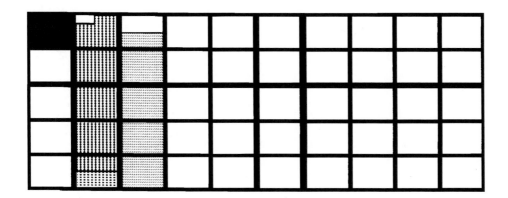

- תרומה	■
- מעשר ראשון	▦
- תרומת מעשר	▦
- מעשר שני	▨

☐ ברכות פרק ז' - שלשה שאכלו - משנה א' חלק א' ☐

1) Three who have eaten together	(1 שְׁלֹשָׁה שֶׁאָכְלוּ כְּאֶחָד
2) are obligated to *bentch* [together].	(2 חַיָּבִין לְזַמֵּן.
3) If he ate questionable* produce,	(3 אָכַל דְּמַאי,
4) or the first *maaser***	(4 וּמַעֲשֵׂר רִאשׁוֹן
5) which has had its [second] *teruma* taken,***	(5 שֶׁנִּטְלָה תְּרוּמָתוֹ,
6) or the second *maaser*,	(6 וּמַעֲשֵׂר שֵׁנִי,
7) or holy [food] which have been redeemed,	(7 וְהֶקְדֵּשׁ שֶׁנִּפְדּוּ,
8) or a waiter who ate a *kezayis*,	(8 וְהַשַּׁמָּשׁ שֶׁאָכַל כְּזַיִת,
9) or a *Kusi*^,	(9 וְהַכּוּתִי,
10) we may *bentch m'zuman* by including them.	(10 מְזַמְּנִין עֲלֵיהֶם.

* *The owner of the produce is not a learned man, therefore we may not assume that he took all* מעשרות *(tithes) properly.*

** *This is the first 1/10 which is removed, it is to be given to a* לֵוִי.

*** *This produce had its second* תרומה *taken [the 1/10 given by the* לוי *to the* כהן*], but its first* תרומה *was not taken.* {*This happened before the storing of the grain was completed.*}

^ *Nowadays a* כּוּתִי *could not be included.*

---

1. Please list the following in the order in which they are supposed to be given:

   מעשר שני, מעשר ראשון, תרומה (גדולה). _____

2. To whom is the תרומה (גדולה) given? _____

3. What percentage of one's crops is given for תרומה (גדולה)? _____ [approximately].

4. To whom is the מעשר ראשון given? _____

5. What percentage of one's crops is given for מעשר ראשון? _____ [exactly].

6. What is done with the מעשר שני? _____

   _____

7. What percentage of the remainder of one's crops is used as מעשר שני? _____

8. How did the Jewish farmers make a living, if they did מצוות with such a large amount of their produce? _____

9. Why might we have thought that the waiter would not be included in the מזומן? _____

☐ ברכות פרק ז' - שלשה שאכלו - משנה א' חלק ב' ☐

1) But	(1 אֲבָל
2) if he ate untithed* produce,	(2 אָכַל טֶבֶל,
3) or the first maaser	(3 וּמַעֲשֵׂר רִאשׁוֹן
4) which did not have its teruma taken,**	(4 שֶׁלֹּא נִטְּלָה תְרוּמָתוֹ,
5) or the second maaser,	(5 וּמַעֲשֵׂר שֵׁנִי,
6) or holy [food] which have not been redeemed,	(6 וְהֶקְדֵּשׁ שֶׁלֹּא נִפְדּוּ,
7) or a waiter who ate less than a kezayis,	(7 וְהַשַּׁמָּשׁ שֶׁאָכַל פָּחוֹת מִכְּזַיִת,
8) or a non-Jew^,	(8 וְהַנָּכְרִי,
9) we may not bentch m'zuman by including them.	(9 אֵין מְזַמְּנִין עֲלֵיהֶם.

* Neither תרומות nor מעשרות were taken from this produce.

** Even though the final storing of the grain took place, and there was an obligation
to give the (גדולה) תרומה, the owner gave the לֵוִי his portion before giving the כהן
the (גדולה) תרומה - therefore there is some (גדולה) תרומה mixed in with the מַעֲשֵׂר רִאשׁוֹן.

^ This משנה is speaking about a non-Jew who had a ברית in order to become Jewish,
but he did not go to the מקוה yet.

_____

1. What is טֶבֶל? _____

_____

2. What is תרומה גדולה? _____

_____

3. What is תְּרוּמַת מַעֲשֵׂר? _____

_____

4. In this case, even though the produce had its second תרומה taken [the 1/10 given by the לוי to the
כהן], it is considered טֶבֶל. What is the difference between this case and the similar case in the first
part of the משנה? _____

_____

5. Why must we say that the נָכְרִי in this משנה is someone who has started to become a גֵר?

⊟ ברכות פרק ז' - שלשה שאכלו - משנה ב' ⊟

1) Women, and slaves,	נָשִׁים, וַעֲבָדִים, (1
2) and minors,	וּקְטַנִּים, (2
3) we may not *bentch m'zuman* by including them.	אֵין מְזַמְּנִין עֲלֵיהֶם. (3
4) Until how little (food)	עַד כַּמָּה (4
5) do we *bentch m'zuman*?	מְזַמְּנִין? (5
6) "Until a *k'zayis*∗."	"עַד כְּזַיִת." (6
7) Rabbe Yehudah says,	רַבִּי יְהוּדָה אוֹמֵר, (7
8) "Until a *k'baitza*^."	"עַד כְּבֵיצָה." (8

∗ *The size of an olive.*

^ *The size of an egg.*

---

1. This משנה is telling us that women cannot make a מזומן together with _____.

2. If a group of women (without men) are eating together, may they *bentch m'zuman*? _____ However, it is not the practice of women to do so.

3. There is a מחלוקת regarding the age of a child who may be included for a מזומן. One opinion says that if he is הִגִּיעַ לְחִנּוּךְ he can be counted for a מזומן. What does הִגִּיעַ לְחִנּוּךְ mean? _____

4. According to the other opinion a boy must be _____ years old to be counted for a מזומן.

5. According to הלכה, how much must a person eat to *bentch* and to be counted for a מזומן? ___

מברך: רבותי נברך.
עונים: יהי שם ה' מברך מעתה ועד עולם.
מברך: יהי שם ה' מברך מעתה ועד עולם.
ברשות מרנן ורבנן ורבותי, נברך*שאכלנו משלו.
עונים: ברוך*שאכלנו משלו ובטובו חיינו.
מברך: ברוך*שאכלנו משלו ובטובו חיינו.
ברוך הוא וברוך שמו.
* (במנין - אלקינו)

⊡ ברכות פרק ז' - שלשה שאכלו - משנה ג' חלק א' ⊡

1) How do they *bentch m'zuman*?   כֵּיצַד מְזַמְּנִין? (1

2) When there are three he says,   בִּשְׁלֹשָׁה אוֹמֵר, (2

3) "Let us bless..."   "נְבָרֵךְ..." (3

4) When there are three and himself he says,   בִּשְׁלֹשָׁה וְהוּא אוֹמֵר, (4

5) "[You] bless..."   "בָּרְכוּ..." (5

6) When there are ten he says,   בַּעֲשָׂרָה אוֹמֵר, (6

7) "Let us bless our G-d..."   "נְבָרֵךְ אֱלֹקֵינוּ..." (7

8) When there are ten and himself he says,   בַּעֲשָׂרָה וְהוּא אוֹמֵר, (8

9) "[You] bless..."   "בָּרְכוּ...." (9

10) One and the same 10 and 10 times 10,000.*   אֶחָד עֲשָׂרָה וְאֶחָד עֲשָׂרָה רִבּוֹא. (10

11) When there are one hundred he says,   בְּמֵאָה אוֹמֵר, (11

12) "Let us bless HaShem our G-d..."   "נְבָרֵךְ ה' אֱלֹקֵינוּ..." (12

13) When there are one hundred and himself he says,   בְּמֵאָה וְהוּא אוֹמֵר, (13

14) "[You] bless..."   "בָּרְכוּ...." (14

15) When there are one thousand he says,   בְּאֶלֶף אוֹמֵר, (15

16) "Let us bless HaShem our G-d, G-d of Yisroel..."   "נְבָרֵךְ לה' אֱלֹקֵינוּ, אֱלֹקֵי יִשְׂרָאֵל..." (16

17) When there are one thousand and himself he says,   בְּאֶלֶף וְהוּא אוֹמֵר, (17

18) "[You] bless..."   "בָּרְכוּ..." (18

★ *This line is the opinion of* רבי עקיבא, *which is found at the end of this* משנה.

---

1. If the מברך (the one who is *bentching*) is needed for the מזומן, he cannot say "ברכו". Why is that? _____

2. According to הלכה, if there are from _____ until _____ men we say, "נברך". If there are _____ or more men we say, "נברך אלקינו".

☐ ברכות פרק ז' - שלשה שאכלו - משנה ג' חלק ב' ☐

1) When there are ten thousand he says,	בְּרִבּוֹא אוֹמֵר, (1
2) "Let us bless HaShem our G-d, G-d of Yisroel,	"נְבָרֵךְ לה' אֱלֹקֵינוּ, אֱלֹקֵי יִשְׂרָאֵל, (2
3) G-d of the Hosts,	אֱלֹקֵי הַצְּבָאוֹת, (3
4) Who sits above the k'ruvim,	יוֹשֵׁב הַכְּרוּבִים, (4
5) for the food which we ate."	עַל הַמָּזוֹן שֶׁאָכַלְנוּ." (5
6) When there are ten thousand and himself he says,	בְּרִבּוֹא וְהוּא אוֹמֵר, (6
7) "[You] bless..."	"בָּרְכוּ...." (7
8) According to the way he blesses	כְּעִנְיָן שֶׁהוּא מְבָרֵךְ (8
9) so they answer after him,	כָּךְ עוֹנִין אַחֲרָיו, (9
10) "Blessed is HaShem our G-d, G-d of Yisroel,	"בָּרוּךְ ה' אֱלֹקֵינוּ, אֱלֹקֵי יִשְׂרָאֵל, (10
11) G-d of the Hosts,	אֱלֹקֵי הַצְּבָאוֹת, (11
12) Who sits above the k'ruvim,	יוֹשֵׁב הַכְּרוּבִים, (12
13) for the food which we ate."	עַל הַמָּזוֹן שֶׁאָכַלְנוּ." (13

---

1. Please draw a line from each word to its translation.

    one hundred   אֶלֶף

    one thousand   מֵאָה

    ten thousand   רִבּוֹא

2. An army, the stars and planets, and the groups of מַלְאָכִים can all be called "הצבאות". What is the meaning of the word "צָבָא"? _____

3. Why is it that the praises which are said for הקב"ה increase as the number of Jews increases?

_____

_____

⊞ בְּרָכוֹת פֶּרֶק ז׳ - שְׁלֹשָׁה שֶׁאָכְלוּ - מִשְׁנָה ג׳ חֵלֶק ג׳ ⊞

1) Rabbe Yossai HaGlili says,	1) רַבִּי יוֹסֵי הַגְּלִילִי אוֹמֵר,
2) "According to the size of the congregation	2) ״לְפִי רוֹב הַקָּהָל
3) they say the brocha.	3) הֵן מְבָרְכִין.
4) Since it says,	4) שֶׁנֶּאֱמַר,
5) 'In groups bless G-d,	5) ׳בְּמַקְהֵלוֹת בָּרְכוּ אֱלֹקִים,
6) HaShem the fountain of Yisroel.'"	6) ה׳ מִמְּקוֹר יִשְׂרָאֵל.׳״
7) Rabbe Akiva said,	7) אָמַר רַבִּי עֲקִיבָא,
8) "How do we find [it] in shul?	8) ״מַה מָּצִינוּ בְּבֵית הַכְּנֶסֶת?
9) One [and the same] many	9) אֶחָד מְרוּבִּין
10) and (one) few say,	10) וְאֶחָד מוּעָטִין אוֹמֵר,
11) '[You] bless HaShem.'"	11) ׳בָּרְכוּ אֶת ה׳.׳״
12) Rabbe Yishmael says,	12) רַבִּי יִשְׁמָעֵאל אוֹמֵר,
13) '[You] bless HaShem Who is blessed.'"	13) ׳בָּרְכוּ אֶת ה׳ הַמְבוֹרָךְ.׳״

1. How does "...בְּמַקְהֵלוֹת בָּרְכוּ אֱלֹקִים" show that the ברכה should increase according to the number of people in the congregation? _____

2. רבי עקיבא says that the פסוק of "...בְּמַקְהֵלוֹת בָּרְכוּ אֱלֹקִים" is referring to the unborn babies singing while they were inside their mothers. When was it that the unborn babies sang? _____

3. What is the reason that רבי ישמעאל admits that the ברכה remains the same in shul, regardless of how many people there are? _____

A shul is for davening, not for catching up on the news.

☐ ברכות פרק ז' - שלשה שאכלו - משנה ד' ☐

1) Three who ate together	שְׁלֹשָׁה שֶׁאָכְלוּ כְּאֶחָד (1
2) they are not permitted to separate,	אֵינָן רַשָׁאִין לַחֲלֹק, (2
3) and so four,	וְכֵן אַרְבָּעָה, (3
4) and so five.	וְכֵן חֲמִשָּׁה. (4
5) Six are permitted to separate	שִׁשָּׁה נֶחֱלָקִין (5
6) - until ten.	עַד עֲשָׂרָה. – (6
7) And ten may not separate	וַעֲשָׂרָה אֵינָן נֶחֱלָקִין (7
8) until there are twenty.	עַד שֶׁיִּהְיוּ עֶשְׂרִים. (8

---

1. What is the reason that three people who ate together may not split up for ברכת המזון? ____

_____

2. What is the reason that five people who ate together may not split up for ברכת המזון? {This is not the same answer as number one.} _____

_____

3. What is the reason that nineteen people who ate together may not split up for ברכת המזון?

_____

4. Please draw a line from each word to its translation.

permitted	שאכלו
to separate	לחלק
that they ate	רשאין

A question to think about...

You are invited to a bar-mitzva, but you don't think that you can stay till bentching. What can you do about bentching מזומן?

⊞ ברכות פרק ז׳ - שלשה שאכלו - משנה ד׳ ⊞

1) Two groups	(1 שְׁתֵּי חֲבוּרוֹת
2) that were eating in one house (room),	(2 שֶׁהָיוּ אוֹכְלוֹת בְּבַיִת אֶחָד,
3) at a time (case) that some of them can see	(3 בִּזְמַן שֶׁמִּקְצָתָן רוֹאִין
4) each other,	(4 אֵלּוּ אֶת אֵלּוּ,
5) they are combined for bentching m'zuman.	(5 מִצְטָרְפִים לְזִמּוּן.
6) And if not,	(6 וְאִם לָאו,
7) these bentch m'zuman for themselves	(7 אֵלּוּ מְזַמְּנִין לְעַצְמָן
8) and these bentch m'zuman for themselves.	(8 וְאֵלּוּ מְזַמְּנִין לְעַצְמָן.
9) "They do not say the brocha* on wine	(9 "אֵין מְבָרְכִין עַל הַיַּיִן
10) until he puts water into it,"	(10 עַד שֶׁיִּתֵּן לְתוֹכוֹ מָיִם,"
11) these are the words of Rabbe Eliezer.	(11 דִּבְרֵי רַבִּי אֱלִיעֶזֶר.
12) And the Chachomim say,	(12 וַחֲכָמִים אוֹמְרִים,
13) "They do say the brocha."	(13 "מְבָרְכִין."

* We are referring to the special ברכה said on wine, "בּוֹרֵא פְּרִי הַגֶּפֶן".

---

1. Often, when the משנה and גמרא say "בית", they do not literally mean "house", but mean

   _____.

2. If one שמש (waiter) serves both groups, they are considered one group, even though _____

   _____

3. For what reason did they pour water into their wine in those days? _____

   _____

4. Is it necessary to put water into the wine we purchase? _____

5. According to רבי אליעזר the ברכה on undiluted wine was בּוֹרֵא פְּרִי הָעֵץ. Why wasn't it

   בּוֹרֵא פְּרִי הַגֶּפֶן? _____

   _____

☐ ברכות פרק ח' - אלו דברים - משנה א' ☐

1) These are the things (differences)	אֵלּוּ דְבָרִים (1
2) which are between Bais Shammai and Bais Hillel	שֶׁבֵּין בֵּית שַׁמַּאי וּבֵית הִלֵּל (2
3) concerning meals.	בַּסְּעוּדָה. (3
4) Bais Shammai say,	בֵּית שַׁמַּאי אוֹמְרִים, (4
5) "He says the *brocha* on the day*	"מְבָרֵךְ עַל הַיּוֹם (5
6) and afterwards he says the *brocha* on the wine.**	וְאַחַר כָּךְ מְבָרֵךְ עַל הַיַּיִן." (6
7) And Bais Hillel say,	וּבֵית הִלֵּל אוֹמְרִים, (7
8) "He says the *brocha* on the wine	"מְבָרֵךְ עַל הַיַּיִן (8
9) and afterwards he says the *brocha* on the day.	וְאַחַר כָּךְ מְבָרֵךְ עַל הַיּוֹם." (9

* *The brocha on the Shabbos or the Yom Tov.*

בורא פרי הגפן **

---

1. בית שמאי say that the ברכה on the day is said first. What do we mean by "the ברכה on the day"? _____

2. Why do בית שמאי say that the ברכה on the day should be said first? [One reason is enough.] _____

3. One of the reasons that בית הלל say the ברכה on the wine should be said first is "תדיר ושאינו תדיר תדיר קודם", what does this mean? _____

4. Please write another reason that בית הלל say the ברכה on the wine should be said first. _____

...בורא פרי הגפן.
...מקדש השבת.

ברכות פרק ח׳ - אלו דברים - משנה ב׳ + ג׳

The הלכות in the following two משניות deal with הלכות of טומאה וטהרה. Most of these הלכות are not in practice today. However, when the בית המקדש will be rebuilt [speedily in our days] these הלכות will be applicable.
The following arguments between בית שמאי ובית הלל are dependent upon their opinions about various הלכות of טומאה וטהרה. For details see the explanation of ר״ע מברטנורא.

◆●◆

1) Bais Shammai say,	בֵּית שַׁמַּאי אוֹמְרִים, (1
2) "They wash [their] hands	"נוֹטְלִין לַיָּדַיִם (2
3) and afterwards they pour the [kiddush] cup."	וְאַחַר כָּךְ מוֹזְגִין אֶת הַכּוֹס." (3
4) And Bais Hillel say,	וּבֵית הַלֵּל אוֹמְרִים, (4
5) "They pour the [kiddush] cup	"מוֹזְגִין אֶת הַכּוֹס (5
6) and afterwards they wash [their] hands."	וְאַחַר כָּךְ נוֹטְלִין לַיָּדַיִם." (6

◆●◆

ברכות פרק ח׳ - אלו דברים - משנה ג׳

1) Bais Shammai say,	בֵּית שַׁמַּאי אוֹמְרִים, (1
2) "He wipes his hands on the towel	"מְקַנֵּחַ יָדָיו בְּמַפָּה (2
3) and places it (the towel) on the table."	וּמַנִּיחַ עַל הַשּׁוּלְחָן." (3
4) And Bais Hillel say,	וּבֵית הַלֵּל אוֹמְרִים, (4
5) "Upon the cushion."	"עַל הַכֶּסֶת." (5

1. Please draw a line from each word to its translation.

they pour	נוֹטְלִין
they wash	מוֹזְגִין
he wipes	מְקַנֵּחַ
towel	מַפָּה

2. Why do בית שמאי say that it is all right to place the damp towel on the table. _____

_____

3. Why do בית הלל say that it is not all right to place the damp towel on the table. _____

_____

🂠 ברכות פרק ח' - אלו דברים - משנה ד' + ה' 🂠

1) Bais Shammai say,	בֵּית שַׁמַּאי אוֹמְרִים, (1
2) "They sweep the house [room]*	"מְכַבְּדִין אֶת הַבַּיִת (2
3) and afterwards they wash [their] hands."	וְאַחַר כָּךְ נוֹטְלִין לַיָּדָיִם." (3
4) And Bais Hillel say,	וּבֵית הִלֵּל אוֹמְרִים, (4
5) "They wash [their] hands	"נוֹטְלִין לַיָּדָיִם (5
6) and afterwards they sweep the house."	וְאַחַר כָּךְ מְכַבְּדִין אֶת הַבַּיִת." (6

🂠 ברכות פרק ח' - אלו דברים - משנה ה' 🂠

1) Bais Shammai say,	בֵּית שַׁמַּאי אוֹמְרִים, (1
2) "[Havdala] candle, bentching,	"נֵר, וּמָזוֹן, (2
3) and spices, and [the brocha of] HaMavdil."	וּבְשָׂמִים, וְהַבְדָּלָה." (3
4) And Bais Hillel say,	וּבֵית הִלֵּל אוֹמְרִים, (4
5) "Candle, & spices, & bentching & Hamavdil."	"נֵר, וּבְשָׂמִים, וּמָזוֹן, וְהַבְדָּלָה." (5
6) Bais Shammai say,	בֵּית שַׁמַּאי אוֹמְרִים, (6
7) "That He created the light of (the) fire."	"שֶׁבָּרָא מְאוֹר הָאֵשׁ." (7
8) And Bais Hillel say,	וּבֵית הִלֵּל אוֹמְרִים, (8
9) "He creates the lights of the fire."	"בּוֹרֵא מְאוֹרֵי הָאֵשׁ." (9

* When the meal is finished, before washing מים אחרונים.

---

1. בית שמאי say that you must make sure to sweep the house [in the area of the table] before washing מים אחרונים, since there may be large pieces of bread [כזית] lying around, and water might fall on the bread. Why should the הלכה "care" if water falls on the bread? _____

   _____

   _____

2. Why does בית הלל assume that there will not be any large pieces of bread lying around? ____

   _____

   _____

🔲 ברכות פרק ח׳ - אלו דברים - משנה ו׳ 🔲

1) We may*not say the brocha	(1	אֵין מְבָרְכִין
2) not on the candle**	(2	לֹא עַל הַנֵּר
3) and not on the spices	(3	וְלֹא עַל הַבְּשָׂמִים
4) of idolaters,	(4	שֶׁל עוֹבְדֵי כּוֹכָבִים,
5) and not on the candle	(5	וְלֹא עַל הַנֵּר
6) and not on the spices	(6	וְלֹא עַל הַבְּשָׂמִים
7) of dead people,	(7	שֶׁל מֵתִים,
8) and not on the candle	(8	וְלֹא עַל הַנֵּר
9) and not on the spices	(9	וְלֹא עַל הַבְּשָׂמִים
10) which are in front of the idols (of idolaters).	(10	שֶׁלִּפְנֵי אֱלִילֵי עוֹבְדֵי כּוֹכָבִים.
11) We may*not say the brocha on the candle	(11	אֵין מְבָרְכִין עַל הַנֵּר
12) until they [can] benefit from its light.	(12	עַד שֶׁיֵּאוֹתוּ לְאוֹרוֹ.

* literally - do not   ** or light

---

1. For what reason can't we say the ברכה on the candle which a non-Jew lit on שבת? ____
   _____

2. For what reason can't we say the ברכה on spices of a non-Jew? _____
   _____

3. The candle which is lit for a dead person is not for the purpose of giving light, but it is lit as an honor for the dead person. Why can't the ברכה be said on this candle? _____
   _____

4. For what reason can't we say the ברכה on spices which are placed near a dead person? ____
   _____

5. What is the משנה teaching when it says, "אֵין מְבָרְכִין עַל הַנֵּר עַד שֶׁיֵּאוֹתוּ לְאוֹרוֹ"? ____
   _____

...בּוֹרֵא מִינֵי בְשָׂמִים.
...בּוֹרֵא מְאוֹרֵי הָאֵשׁ.

⊟ ברכות פרק ח׳ - אלו דברים - משנה ז׳ ⊟

1) One who ate	(1 מִי שֶׁאָכַל
2) and forgot to *bentch*,*	(2 וְשָׁכַח וְלֹא בֵּירֵךְ,
3) Bais Shammai say,	(3 בֵּית שַׁמַּאי אוֹמְרִים,
4) "He must return to his place and *bentch*."	(4 ״יַחֲזוֹר לִמְקוֹמוֹ וִיבָרֵךְ.״
5) And Bais Hillel say,	(5 וּבֵית הִלֵּל אוֹמְרִים,
6) "He [may] *bentch* in the place where he remembered."	(6 ״יְבָרֵךְ בַּמָּקוֹם שֶׁנִּזְכַּר.״
7) Until when may he *bentch*?	(7 עַד אֵימָתַי הוּא מְבָרֵךְ?
8) Until	(8 עַד כְּדֵי
9) the food in his stomach is digested.	(9 שֶׁיִּתְעַכֵּל הַמָּזוֹן שֶׁבְּמֵעָיו.

* literally - and did not *bentch*

---

1. According to בית הלל is a person allowed to leave the place where he ate, and *bentch* in another place? _____

2. If a person ate a light meal, until when can he *bentch*? _____

3. If a person ate a heavy meal, until when can he *bentch*? _____

---

4. Please draw a line from each word to its translation.

he forgot	שכך
he must return	אימתי
when	יחזור

◻ ברכות פרק ח׳ - אלו דברים - משנה ח׳ ◻

1)	If wine was brought to them after the meal	(1 בָּא לָהֶם יַיִן לְאַחַר הַמָּזוֹן
2)	and there isn't [wine] there except that cup,	(2 וְאֵין שָׁם אֶלָּא אוֹתוֹ הַכּוֹס,
3)	Bais Shammai say,	(3 בֵּית שַׁמַּאי אוֹמְרִים,
4)	"He may say the *brocha* on the wine	(4 ״מְבָרֵךְ עַל הַיַּיִן
5)	and afterwards (he should) *bentch*."	(5 וְאַחַר כָּךְ מְבָרֵךְ עַל הַמָּזוֹן.״
6)	And Bais Hillel say,	(6 וּבֵית הִלֵּל אוֹמְרִים,
7)	"He should *bentch*	(7 ״מְבָרֵךְ עַל הַמָּזוֹן
8)	and afterwards	(8 וְאַחַר כָּךְ
9)	he should say the *brocha* on the wine."	(9 מְבָרֵךְ עַל הַיַּיִן.״
10)	We answer "Amen"	(10 עוֹנִין אָמֵן
11)	after a Jew who says a *brocha*,	(11 אַחַר יִשְׂרָאֵל הַמְבָרֵךְ,
12)	and we don't answer "Amen"	(12 וְאֵין עוֹנִין אָמֵן
13)	after a *Kusi* who says a *brocha*	(13 אַחַר כּוּתִי הַמְבָרֵךְ
14)	until he hears	(14 עַד שֶׁיִּשְׁמַע
15)	the entire *brocha* (entirely).	(15 כָּל הַבְּרָכָה כּוּלָהּ.

---

1. According to the opinion of this משנה, Bais Shammai holds that ברכת המזון does not need a

   כוס. Therefore, if he would like to drink the wine before _____, he may.

2. According to the opinion of בית הלל we must have wine for ברכת המזון. Therefore, _____

   _____

3. Who were the כותים? _____

   _____

4. Why was it necessary to hear the entire ברכה before answering אמן to the ברכה of a כותי?

   _____

5. After the חכמים stated that the כותים are like 100% idolators, it became אסור to answer

   אמן to a ברכה said by a כותי, even if we heard the entire ברכה. Why is this? _____

> It is necessary to speak to a Rav before putting הלכות which you learn in a משנה
> into practice.   Regarding ברכות which are not commonly said,
> it is certainly necessary to speak to your Rav.

☐ ברכות פרק ט׳ - הרואה - משנה א׳ ☐

1) One who sees a place	הָרוֹאֶה מָקוֹם	(1
2) where miracles were done for Yisroel	שֶׁנַּעֲשׂוּ בּוֹ נִסִּים לְיִשְׂרָאֵל	(2
3) says,	אוֹמֵר,	(3
4) "Boruch... Who did miracles for our fathers	"בָּרוּךְ שֶׁעָשָׂה נִסִּים לַאֲבוֹתֵינוּ	(4
5) in this place."	בַּמָּקוֹם הַזֶּה."	(5
6) [If he sees] a place in Eretz Yisroel	מָקוֹם בְּאֶרֶץ יִשְׂרָאֵל	(6
7) that from it was uprooted	שֶׁנֶּעֶקְרָה מִמֶּנּוּ	(7
8) idolatry	עֲבוֹדַת כּוֹכָבִים	(8
9) he says,	אוֹמֵר	(9
10) "Boruch... Who uprooted idolatry	"בָּרוּךְ שֶׁעָקַר עֲבוֹדַת כּוֹכָבִים	(10
11) from our land."	מֵאַרְצֵנוּ."	(11

---

1. Which part of a ברכה is the "שֵׁם וּמַלְכוּת"?

(A) ה׳ אלקינו מלך העולם   (B) ברוך אתה ה׳   (C) אשר קדשנו במצותיו וצונו

2. A ברכה which is said upon the fulfillment of a מצוה is called a ברכת המצוות.   Which words

show us that a ברכה is being said upon the fulfillment of a מצוה?

(A) ה׳ אלקינו מלך העולם   (B) ברוך אתה ה׳   (C) אשר קדשנו במצותיו וצונו

3. If you see a place where a private נס was done for a person, do you say a ברכה?

_____

4. Which [three] people would say a ברכה in the place where a private נס happened? _____

_____

_____

5. In which case would a person say "ברוך שעקר עבודת כוכבים ממקום הזה"? _____

☐ בְּרָכוֹת פֶּרֶק ט׳ - הָרוֹאֶה - מִשְׁנָה ב׳ ☐

1)	Over comets [or meteors], & over earthquakes,	עַל הַזִּיקִין, וְעַל הַזְּוָעוֹת,	(1
2)	& over lightning, & over thunder,	וְעַל הַבְּרָקִים, וְעַל הָרְעָמִים,	(2
3)	& over [violent] winds he says,	וְעַל הָרוּחוֹת אוֹמֵר,	(3
4)	"Boruch... Whose power & strength fill the world."	״בָּרוּךְ שֶׁכֹּחוֹ וּגְבוּרָתוֹ מָלֵא עוֹלָם.״	(4
5)	Over the mountains, and over the hills,	עַל הֶהָרִים, וְעַל הַגְּבָעוֹת,	(5
6)	and over the seas, and over the rivers,	וְעַל הַיַּמִּים, וְעַל הַנְּהָרוֹת,	(6
7)	and over the wildernesses he says,	וְעַל הַמִּדְבָּרוֹת אוֹמֵר,	(7
8)	"Boruch... Who makes the work of Creation."	״בָּרוּךְ עוֹשֶׂה מַעֲשֵׂה בְרֵאשִׁית.״	(8
9)	Rabbe Yehuda says,	רַבִּי יְהוּדָה אוֹמֵר,	(9
10)	"One who sees the Great Sea says,	״הָרוֹאֶה אֶת הַיָּם הַגָּדוֹל אוֹמֵר,	(10
11)	'Boruch... Who made the Great Sea,'	׳בָּרוּךְ שֶׁעָשָׂה אֶת הַיָּם הַגָּדוֹל,׳	(11
12)	[but] only if he sees it from time to time."	בִּזְמַן שֶׁרוֹאֶה אוֹתוֹ לִפְרָקִים.״	(12
13)	On the rains	עַל הַגְּשָׁמִים	(13
14)	and on the good tidings (news) he says,	וְעַל הַבְּשׂוֹרוֹת הַטּוֹבוֹת אוֹמֵר,	(14
15)	"Boruch... He Who is good and does good."	״בָּרוּךְ הַטּוֹב וְהַמֵּטִיב.״	(15
16)	And on bad tidings (news) he says,	וְעַל שְׁמוּעוֹת רָעוֹת אוֹמֵר,	(16
17)	"Boruch... the true Judge."	״בָּרוּךְ דַּיַּן הָאֱמֶת.״	(17

---

1. Which בְּרָכָה do we say on lightning? _____

2. According to some opinions the יָם הַגָּדוֹל is the _____ Ocean. According to other opinions it is the _____ Sea.

3. The בְּרָכוֹת on seeing special places are not said if you see the place often. If you did not see the place for _____ days you do say the בְּרָכָה.

⊟ בְּרָכוֹת פֶּרֶק ט' - הָרוֹאֶה - מִשְׁנָה ג' ⊟

1) If he built a new house,	(1 בָּנָה בַּיִת חָדָשׁ,
2) or if he bought new objects,	(2 וְקָנָה כֵּלִים חֲדָשִׁים,
3) he says, "Boruch SheHecheyanu."	(3 אוֹמֵר, "בָּרוּךְ שֶׁהֶחֱיָנוּ."
4) He says a brocha on the bad,	(4 מְבָרֵךְ עַל הָרָעָה,
5) within the good;*	(5 מֵעֵין הַטּוֹבָה;
6) and on the good within the bad.	(6 וְעַל הַטּוֹבָה מֵעֵין הָרָעָה.
7) One who cries out about the past,	(7 הַצּוֹעֵק לְשֶׁעָבַר,
8) behold this is a t'fila for nothing.	(8 הֲרֵי זוֹ תְּפִלַּת שָׁוְא.
9) How is this?	(9 כֵּיצַד?
10) If his wife was pregnant,	(10 הָיְתָה אִשְׁתּוֹ מְעֻבֶּרֶת,
11) and he said, "May it be His Will	(11 וְאָמַר, "יְהִי רָצוֹן
12) that my wife should give birth to a male,"	(12 שֶׁתֵּלֵד אִשְׁתִּי זָכָר,"
13) behold this is	(13 הֲרֵי זוֹ
14) a t'fila for nothing.	(14 תְּפִלַּת שָׁוְא.
15) If he was (coming) on the way	(15 הָיָה בָא בַּדֶּרֶךְ
16) and he heard the sound of crying in the city	(16 וְשָׁמַע קוֹל צְוָחָה בָּעִיר
17) and said,	(17 וְאָמַר,
18) "May it be His will that these should not be	(18 "יְהִי רָצוֹן שֶׁלֹּא יִהְיוּ אֵלּוּ
19) the members of my household,"	(19 בְּנֵי בֵיתִי,"
20) behold this is	(20 הֲרֵי זוֹ
21) a t'fila for nothing.	(21 תְּפִלַּת שָׁוְא.

★ SOMETHING WHICH IS BAD NOW, BUT WILL TURN OUT GOOD.

---

1) If your family bought expensive new furniture, is a שהחינו said? _____

2) If someone gave you very nice used clothes (a "hand-me-down") that you are very happy to receive, do you say a ברכה? _____ Which ברכה? _____

3) If his field was ruined by a flood, but the mud will be good for his field next year, which ברכה does he say? _____

◻ ברכות פרק ט' - הרואה - משנה ד' ◻

1)	One who enters a city*	הַנִּכְנָס לִכְרַךְ	(1
2)	should *daven* [for safety] twice,	מִתְפַּלֵּל שְׁתַּיִם,	(2
3)	once when he enters	אַחַת בִּכְנִיסָתוֹ	(3
4)	and once when he leaves.	וְאַחַת בִּיצִיאָתוֹ.	(4
5)	Ben Azai says,	בֶּן עַזַּאי אוֹמֵר,	(5
6)	"Twice when he enters	"שְׁתַּיִם בִּכְנִיסָתוֹ	(6
7)	and twice when he leaves.**	וּשְׁתַּיִם בִּיצִיאָתוֹ.	(7
8)	- (And) he gives thanks for what is past,	וְנוֹתֵן הוֹדָאָה לְשֶׁעָבַר, -	(8
9)	and cries out about what will happen."	וְצוֹעֵק לֶעָתִיד לָבֹא."	(9

* *The city is run by people who are harsh towards Jews.*

** *The* משנה *will now explain that there is a* תפלה *of request and a* תפלה *of*
appeciation both upon entering and upon leaving. This adds up to four תפלות.

---

1. Please draw a line from each word to its translation.

    one who enters   הנכנס

    when he leaves   בכניסתו

    when he enters   ביציאתו

2. What does the משנה mean by "הודאה"? _____

_____

3. What does the משנה mean by "(צועק) צעקה"? _____

_____

כללו של דבר: לעולם יצעק אדם על העתיד לבא ויבקש רחמים ויתן הודיה על מה שעבר
ויודה וישבח כפי כחו. וכל המרבה להודות את ה' ולשבחו תמיד הרי זה משובח.
רמב"ס סוף פרק י' מהלכות ברכות

☐ ברכות פרק ט' - הרואה - משנה ה' חלק א' ☐

1) A man is obligated to "bless"	1) חַיָּב אָדָם לְבָרֵךְ
2) for bad things	2) עַל הָרָעָה
3) just like he must bless	3) כְּשֵׁם שֶׁהוּא מְבָרֵךְ
4) for good things-	4) עַל הַטּוֹבָה-
5) Since it says, "You should love HaShem	5) שֶׁנֶּאֱמַר, "וְאָהַבְתָּ אֵת הַשֵּׁם
6) your G-d with your entire mind,	6) אֱלֹקֶיךָ בְּכָל לְבָבְךָ,
7) and your entire life, & all your money."	7) וּבְכָל נַפְשְׁךָ, וּבְכָל מְאֹדֶךָ."
8) 'with your entire heart'-	8) 'בְּכָל לְבָבְךָ'-
9) with your two FORCES-	9) בִּשְׁנֵי יְצָרֶיךָ-
10) with the *Yetzer Tov* & the *Yetzer Ra*.	10) בְּיֵצֶר טוֹב וּבְיֵצֶר רָע.
11) 'And with your entire life'-	11) 'וּבְכָל נַפְשְׁךָ'-
12) even if He is taking	12) אֲפִילוּ הוּא נוֹטֵל
13) your life.	13) אֵת נַפְשְׁךָ.
14) 'And with all your fortune'-	14) 'וּבְכָל מְאֹדֶךָ'-
15) [this means] with all your money.	15) בְּכָל מָמוֹנְךָ.

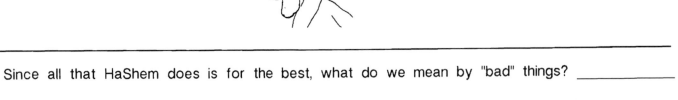

---

1) Since all that HaShem does is for the best, what do we mean by "bad" things? _____

_____

2) What is the meaning of the ברכה of דַּיָּן הָאֱמֶת? _____

_____

3) Up till how much money must we spend to fulfill a מִצְוַת עֲשֵׂה? _____

4) What are the TWO forces in every person? _____

☐ ברכות פרק ט׳ - הרואה - משנה ה׳ חלק ב׳ ☐

1) Another explanation,	דָּבָר אַחֵר,	(1
2) "with all your fortune"-	״בְּכָל מְאֹדֶךָ״-	(2
3) with every measure and measure*	בְּכָל מִדָּה וּמִדָּה	(3
4) that He measures (out) for you,	שֶׁהוּא מוֹדֵד לְךָ,	(4
5) you should thank (admit to) Him	הֱוֵי מוֹדֶה לוֹ	(5
6) [very, very much].	[בִּמְאֹד מְאֹד].	(6

7) A person should not be light-headed**	לֹא יָקֵל אָדָם אֶת רֹאשׁוֹ	(7
8) opposite the eastern gate,	כְּנֶגֶד שַׁעַר הַמִּזְרָח,	(8
9) since it is opposite	שֶׁהוּא מְכֻוָּן כְּנֶגֶד	(9
10) the Holy of Holies.	בֵּית קָדְשֵׁי הַקֳּדָשִׁים.	(10
11) A person must not enter the Temple Mount	לֹא יִכָּנֵס לְהַר הַבַּיִת	(11
12) with his walking stick and his shoes,	בְּמַקְלוֹ וּבְמִנְעָלָיו,	(12
13) and with his money belt,	וּבְפֻנְדָּתוֹ,	(13
14) and with the dust on his feet.	וּבְאָבָק שֶׁעַל רַגְלָיו.	(14
15) And he shouldn't make it	וְלֹא יַעֲשֶׂנּוּ	(15
16) (into a) short-cut,	קַפַּנְדַּרְיָא,	(16
17) or an expectorant (a place to spit)	וּרְקִיקָה	(17
18) from a *kal v'chomer* (obvious rule).	מִקַּל וָחֹמֶר.	(18

* GOOD OR WHAT SEEMS BAD   ** JOKE AROUND ETC.

---

1) What does גם זו לטובה mean? _____

2) A shul is called a מִקְדָּשׁ מְעַט. What should we learn from this משנה in regard to a בית כנסת? _____

3) Does the law of קפנדריא apply in a shul? _____

4) How can you go into a shul to tell someone he has a phone call? _____

⊞ ברכות פרק ט׳ - הרואה - משנה ה׳ חלק ג׳ ⊞

1) At the endings of all *brochos*		כָּל חוֹתְמֵי בְרָכוֹת	(1
2) that were in the Bais-HaMikdash,		שֶׁהָיוּ בַמִּקְדָּשׁ,	(2
3) they said,		הָיוּ אוֹמְרִים,	(3
4) "From the Beginning".*		״מִן הָעוֹלָם״.	(4
5) From when the *Minin* made problems		מִשֶּׁקִּלְקְלוּ הַמִּינִין	(5
6) and said, "There is No world		וְאָמְרוּ, ״אֵין עוֹלָם	(6
7) except for one,"**		אֶלָּא אֶחָד,״	(7
8) they decreed that they should say,		הִתְקִינוּ שֶׁיְּהוּ אוֹמְרִים,	(8
9) "From the 'world' until the 'world'."		״מִן הָעוֹלָם וְעַד הָעוֹלָם.״	(9

---

10) And they (also) decreed,		וְהִתְקִינוּ,	(10
11) that a person should ask		שֶׁיְּהֵא אָדָם שׁוֹאֵל	(11
12) how his friend is		אֶת שְׁלוֹם חֲבֵירוֹ	(12
13) with HaShem's Name;		בְּשֵׁם;	(13
14) since it says, "And behold Boaz is coming		שֶׁנֶּאֱמַר, ״וְהִנֵּה בֹעַז בָּא	(14
15) from Bais Lechem,		מִבֵּית לֶחֶם,	(15
16) and he said to the reapers (grain cutters),		וַיֹּאמֶר לַקּוֹצְרִים,	(16
17) 'HaShem should be with you,'		׳הַשֵּׁם עִמָּכֶם,׳	(17
18) and they said to him,		וַיֹּאמְרוּ לוֹ,	(18
19) '[HaShem] He should bless you'."		׳יְבָרֶכְךָ [הַשֵּׁם].׳״	(19

    * THE BEGINNING OF THE WORLD   ** עוֹלָם הַזֶּה

---

1) Where would you hear a בְּרָכָה ended as follows, ״בָּרוּךְ הַשֵּׁם אֱלֹקֵי יִשְׂרָאֵל מִן הָעוֹלָם וְעַד

    הָעוֹלָם חוֹנֵן הַדָּעַת.״ _____

2) Why did we begin to add, ״וְעַד הָעוֹלָם״? _____

⊡ ברכות פרק ט׳ - הרואה - משנה ה׳ חלק ד׳ ⊡

We are now continuing to prove that it was proper for בועז to decree that people

should greet each other with the Name of הקב״ה.

1) And it [also] says,	וְאוֹמֵר,	(1
2) "HaShem is with you man of valor."	"ה׳ עִמְּךָ גִּבּוֹר הֶחָיִל."	(2
3) And it also says,	וְאוֹמֵר,	(3
4) "And do not despise [your mother]	"וְאַל תָּבוּז	(4
5) because your mother has become old."	כִּי זָקְנָה אִמֶּךָ."	(5
6) And it also says,	וְאוֹמֵר,	(6
7) "It is a time for HaShem to act (punish)	"עֵת לַעֲשׂוֹת לה׳	(7
8) they have made the law* void."	הֵפֵרוּ תוֹרָתֶךָ."	(8
9) Rabbe Nosson says,	רַבִּי נָתָן אוֹמֵר,	(9
10) "They voided the Torah -	"הֵפֵרוּ תוֹרָתֶךָ -	(10
11) it is a time to act for HaShem."	עֵת לַעֲשׂוֹת לה׳."	(11

    * *Ancient customs are also referred to as "law" here.*

_____

1. What are we trying to prove from "ה׳ עִמְּךָ גִּבּוֹר הֶחָיִל" [when the מלאך gave a ברכה to גדעון? _____

2. Which פסוק teaches that we should not <u>despise</u> מנהגים which our ancestors made long ago?

_____

3. Which lines in the משנה teach that it is very wrong to void (make like nothing) the laws of the תורה, and the laws of the חכמים, and even ancient מנהגים? _____

4. רבי נתן says that the פסוק of, "...הֵפֵרוּ תוֹרָתֶךָ" shows us that בועז felt that he should introduce the idea of people greeting each other with the name of השם, even though it may look like people were saying _____.

סליק מסכת ברכות

ANSWER SHEETS

Numbered according to top left of each page.

PAGE #27

1. מדרבנן.
2. Since these items are very special, we should give a special thanks for them.
3. האדמה.
4. Since the branch does not live to produce a second crop of bananas.

PAGE #28

1. עץ, אילן.
2. Since it also grows from the ground.
3. Since they do not grow from a tree.
4. Yes.
5. No.
6. Say a העץ on a plum and a האדמה on a potato chip.
7. Call someone up on the phone and ask him what the proper ברכה is.

PAGE #29

1. שהכל.
2. Since they do not get their nourishment from the ground in the way other plants do.
3. Since they fell off the tree before they were ripe.
4. Since wine that spoils becomes vinegar.
5. Since they destroy the crops. {Some people say that only something which was once good and then spoiled is considered a מין קללה, if so locusts would not be considered a מין קללה.}
6. Since we are not certain which types are kosher.

PAGE #30

1. Wheat and barley.
2. The other types of grain are considered part of the wheat and barley groups.
3. An X with a line going through it, then two straight lines.
4. The grapes.
5. Whichever he [normally] likes more.

PAGE #31

1. Yes.
2. Since both the פרפרת and the bread are made from flour.
3. Something made of flour which is cooked.

PAGE #32

1. When they recline they become one group, therefore one person can say the ברכה for everyone.
2. Let us go and eat bread in that place.
3. המוציא.
4. Since some people might have food in their mouths.
5. סברי מרנן... (So that everyone should finish what is in his mouth and pay attention.)

PAGE #33

1. The item he really wants to eat.
2. The item which he is eating as an aid.
3. The מליח is too salty.
4. Make a מוציא.

PAGE #34

1. Three (and one more from the rabbis).
2. The רבנן added the fourth ברכה.
3. על המחיה.
4. To swallow a pill. The doctor told you to drink for your health.
5. Before drinking water.

PAGE #35

1. א' תרומה (גדולה), ב' מעשר ראשון, ג' מעשר שני.
2. A כהן.
3. 2% which is the same as 1/50.
4. A לוי.
5. 10% which is the same as 1/10.
6. Either the owner takes it to ירושלים, or he redeems it for money which he uses to buy food in ירושלים (which he eats there).
7. 10% which is the same as 1/10.
8. השם made them much more successful since they did the מצוות.
9. Since he does not sit down to eat in a set way.

PAGE #36

1. Produce which did not have the proper תרומות and מעשרות removed.
2. The 1/50 which is given to a כהן.
3. 1/10 which the לוי takes from his מעשר to give to a כהן.

4. Since the preparations for storing the grain had been completed, the grain is obligated in תרומה. Since the לוי took his portion before the תרומה was removed, there is תרומה mixed in with the לוי's portion.

5. Otherwise it would be obvious that he can't be counted for the מזומן.

PAGE #37

1. Men.
2. Yes.
3. He has reached the age at which he should be trained in doing מצוות.
4. 13.
5. A כזית (the size of an olive).

PAGE #38

1. Since the word "ברכו" gives instructions to <u>other</u> people, but without himself there aren't enough for a מזומן.
2. 3, 9, 10.

PAGE #39

1. An X with a line underneath.
2. A large group of powerful things.
3. When more Jews serve השם the קדוש השם is much greater.

PAGE #40

1. The word "מקהלות" means groups. Therefore the פסוק is telling us that according to the [size] of the group השם will be praised.
2. When we crossed the ים סוף.
3. Since the חזן is usually not aware of the exact number of people in the shul.

PAGE #41

1. Since they will not have a מזומן any longer.
2. Since one of the groups will not have a מזומן any longer.
3. Since one of the groups will not have a מזומן for the word אלקינו any longer.
4. An X with a line through it.

{If you are invited to a בר מצוה, but cannot stay till the end - Don't eat bread. **OR** Ask nine other people to *bentch* with you <u>(being careful not to disturb anyone)</u>. **OR** Don't become a part of the group when you begin to eat.}

PAGE #42

1. Room.
2. The two groups cannot see each other.
3. The wine was too strong to drink undiluted.
4. No.
5. Since it is not in its best form, it does not get the best ברכה.

PAGE #43

1. The ברכה on the holiness of Shabbos or Yom Tov.
2. Since it is the day that makes you obligated to make קדוש. **OR** Since the day began before you make the ברכות.
3. What is said more often is said first.
4. Since if you did not have the wine you would not be able to make קדוש.

PAGE #44

1. An X and then two straight lines.
2. בית שמאי opine that it is אסור to use a table that is טמא, therefore the damp towel will not become טמא if placed on the table.
3. בית הלל opine that it is מותר to use a table that is טמא, therefore the damp towel may become טמא if placed on the table.

PAGE #45

1. We are not allowed to spoil food which is a כזית, and if dirty water gets on it people won't want to eat it. (It is a good thing to be careful even with pieces which are smaller than a כזית.)
2. בית הלל opine that you may not use a waiter who is unlearned. Since your waiter will know the הלכה, you can assume that he removed any piece which is a כזית (from the area which may get wet).

PAGE #46

1. The הבדלה flame must have been "resting" on Shabbos.
2. Since it was very common to use their spices for idolatry.
3. Since the flame must be burning for the purpose of giving benefit.
4. Since their purpose is the removal of the odor, not to give a pleasant odor.
5. That the flame must be large enough to give beneficial light.

PAGE #47

1. No.
2. 72 minutes.
3. Until he is no longer satisfied from having eaten that meal.
4. A line across, then an X.

PAGE #48

1. ברכת המזון.
2. He must save the wine for ברכת המזון.
3. Non-Jews who became Jewish out of fear since they were attacked by lions. They did not observe all of the מצוות and were declared to be non-Jews when it was discovered that they worshiped an idol on Har Grizim, where they lived.
4. Since we would not know if they were saying the ברכה to HaShem, unless we heard the entire ברכה.
5. Since his intentions would probably be wrong.

PAGE #49

1. A.
2. C.
3. No.
4. The person, his descendants, and his תלמידים.
5. Outside of ארץ ישראל.

PAGE #50

1. עושה מעשה בראשית.
2. Atlantic. Mediterranean.
3. 30.

PAGE #51

1. No. [You would say הטוב והמטיב, you would say שהחינו only if it was for your own exclusive use.]
2. Yes. שהחינו.
3. דין האמת.

PAGE #52

1. A line across, then an X.
2. Thanking HaShem for what He has done for you.
3. Davening to HaShem for help.

PAGE #53

1. Things which appear to be bad.
2. HaShem is the True Judge.
3. One fifth.
4. The יצר הרע and the יצר הטוב.

PAGE #54

1. This is also for the best.
2. To treat a shul with the utmost respect.
3. Yes.
4. Stop in the shul to learn a little.

PAGE #55

1. In the בית המקדש.
2. Since the מינין were saying that there is no עולם הבא.

PAGE #56

1. That the Name of HaShem is used in giving a greeting.
2. ואל תבוז כי זקנה אמך.
3. 7 & 8.
4. HaShem's Name in vain.

Made in United States
North Haven, CT
30 April 2023

36087131R00020